THE
GOLDEN RULES
OF
FISHING

HA! HA!

CORGI BOOKS

KV-016-042

THE GOLDEN RULES OF FISHING

A CORGI BOOK 0 552 12596 2

First publication in Great Britain

PRINTING HISTORY
Corgi edition published 1985
Corgi edition reissued 1985

Corgi Books are published by Transworld Publishers Ltd.,
Century House, 61-63 Uxbridge Road, Ealing, London W5 5SA,
in Australia by Transworld Publishers (Aust.) Pty. Ltd.,
26 Harley Crescent, Condell Park, NSW 2200, and in New
Zealand by Transworld Publishers (N.Z.) Ltd., Cnr. Moselle
and Waipareira Avenues, Henderson, Auckland.

Made and printed in Great Britain by
Hunt Barnard Printing Ltd., Aylesbury, Bucks.

Always test the flexibility of any rod before purchasing it.

Bread can be a very successful groundbait when fishing for chub and barbel. Make sure to throw it in the right place.

Carry spares withyou at all time, as a days' fishing could be ruined if you lose or break an important piece of tackle.

It is advisable to practise casting a fly when and wherever possible.

A tackle trolley can be very useful, but only use it if ground conditions are suitable.

Be careful when using a trident as it can be dangerous if used improperly.

The essence of good enjoyable fishing is to feel comfortable and to have everything at hand.

Be extremely cautious if you have to break ice to fish. The dangers are obvious.

Apart from keeping out the rain, an umbrella is a superb wind-break and is a necessary part of your equipment.

When unhooking a fish, make certain that you do not damage either the fish or yourself.

Stand on something firm and non-slippery when fishing from the water.

Always cast with the wind behind you.

When float fishing always determine the depth of water you intend fishing, as this will enable you to fix the float in the correct position.

Pork luncheon meat is one of the best ways to entice chub and barbel onto your hook.

When fishing from the shore, a beach rod rest and a beach shelter are invaluable when taking quick breaks.

It is vital that all fish are humanely killed.

Never use a gaff when fishing from an inflatable craft.

When standing in water make certain that boots or waders are of adequate height.

If your hook or line become snagged in a tree, it may be easier to cut the line than try to release it.

Always return small fish to the water as quickly as possible.

When fishing alone in a boat, ensure that the craft is well-anchored.

Never fish stretches which are privately owned, except with prior permission. Some owners can become annoyed.

If you use a gaff, take special precautions especially when wandering along the bank with it.

It is essential to carry a torch when night fishing.

Be courteous and respectful at all times to any other persons who are fishing.

If a hook lodges in your ear, hand or elsewhere on your person, it is advisable to seek help in dislodging it.

A rod licence allows you to fish with ONE rod only.

The old or infirm should be especially diligent as regards to safety near the water.

When casting, make sure that no person is in close proximity.

It is unreasonable behaviour to fish too closely to another angler. There are always good fishing spots nearby.

If you feel that your catch may be a record, get it weighed in front of witnesses as soon as possible.

If more than one person is casting from a boat extra care should be taken.

Tackle should be bought only from a reputable dealer.

As worm bait is expensive, it makes sense and is a simple task to dig your own lugworm bait.

Try to identify any catch, and inform the relevant authorities if you feel that it may be of interest to them.

Never look behind you whilst casting a fly.

Strap yourself securely to your seat when deep-sea fishing for large species.

It is essential to get your lightweight hookbait samples out a long way. Find a method that will suit you.

Salmon must be caught only with hook and line, and must not be taken out of season.

Always keep any noise to an absolute minimum as fish have acute hearing.

It is advisable not to take a dog whilst fishing. They can be a nuisance to you and others and scare away any fish.

Putting together a three piece rod is straightforward if this procedure is followed. First fix the top joint into the middle. Push firmly, then add the butt to the middle and top joint section.

It is essential to stand in a comfortable position when casting.

The grip should always be easy when casting a fly.

Keep as fit as you are able, as playing a fish for a long time needs patience and stamina and can become very tiring.